macaroons

macaroons

30 recipes for perfect bite-size treats

First published in 2011
LOVE FOOD is an imprint of Parragon Books Ltd

Parragon
Queen Street House
4 Queen Street
Bath BA1 1HE, UK

Copyright © Parragon Books Ltd 2011

ISBN: 978-1-4454-2206-0

Printed in China

All photography by Clive Streeter, except front cover (© Cindy Loughridge/Getty Images)
Recipes and home economy by Angela Drake

Notes for the Reader
This book uses imperial, metric, and US cup measurements. Follow the same units of
measurement throughout; do not mix imperial and metric. All spoon measurements are
level: teaspoons are assumed to be 5 ml, and tablespoons are assumed to be 15 ml. Unless
otherwise stated, milk is assumed to be whole, individual vegetables are medium, eggs are
large, and pepper is freshly ground black pepper.

The times given are an approximate guide only. Preparation times differ according to the
techniques used by different people and the cooking times may also vary from those
given as a result of the type of oven used. Optional ingredients, variations, or serving
suggestions have not been included in the calculations.

Recipes using raw or very lightly cooked eggs should be avoided by infants, the elderly,
pregnant women, convalescents, and anyone with a chronic condition. Pregnant and
breast-feeding women are advised to avoid eating peanuts and peanut products. People
with nut allergies should be aware that some of the prepared ingredients used in the
recipes in this book may contain nuts. Always check the package before use.

Contents

Introduction

French *macarons* or macaroons are small almond meringues sandwiched together with a flavored filling to make delightful bite-size treats. Made from egg whites, ground almonds, and superfine and confectioners' sugars, they are characterized by their smooth domed tops, frilly edged bottoms, and wonderfully soft and slightly chewy centers. Popular in French patisseries, where a dazzling array of colors and flavors can be found, macaroons are the perfect after-dinner treat, sweet gift, teatime indulgence, or wedding favor.

As simple as they look, macaroons can be a little tricky to make—indeed, pastry chefs can spend years perfecting the art of macaroons. However, don't let that put you off because this book has everything you need to know for successful macaroon making—from a guide to the essential equipment and ingredients you will need, to clear and detailed step-by-step instructions for the basic method used to make all the macaroons in the book.

Once you've mastered the basic technique, you can try any of the 30 deliciously different macaroons in this book. From classic flavors, such as vanilla, chocolate, and pistachio, to more unusual combinations, such as sesame and lime or even peanut butter and jelly, you'll be spoiled with so many choices.

So what are you waiting for? You may not quite achieve the high standards of a French pastry chef with your first few batches, but with practice and patience you will soon find that the art of making macaroons is a pleasurable pastime with the most fabulous results!

- If your piping skills are not too good, mark circles on the parchment paper by dipping a small cookie cutter or the end of a large piping tip into confectioners' sugar and tapping it onto the paper. However, it's not a problem if the circles vary in size—just match them up according to size when pairing them together.

- Use the oven temperature stated in the recipes as a guide—once you have made a couple of batches of macaroons, you may find that the temperature of your oven needs reducing or increasing a little to achieve the best results. Use an oven thermometer if you have one. Fan ovens cook more quickly than conventional ovens, so reduce the temperature by 50–68°F/10–20°C. You may also find they cook the macaroons a little quicker—usually in about 9–10 minutes.

- If you find the bottoms of the macaroons are browning too quickly, place the baking sheet on a second baking sheet to diffuse the heat. If the tops of the macaroons crack, the oven temperature is too high.

- If the macaroons shells stick to the parchment paper, try spraying a little water between the paper and baking sheet to create a little steam, which will help to release them.

- Unfilled macaroons will keep for 3–4 days in an airtight container or freeze for up to 1 month. Filled macaroons will keep in the refrigerator for 2–3 days, depending on the type of filling. They are best eaten at room temperature a few hours after filling.

10 Steps to Macaroon Perfection

Refer to this simple step-by-step guide when making any of the macaroon recipes in this book.

STEP 1: Place the ground almonds and confectioners' sugar in a food processor and process for about 15 seconds, until the mixture is fine and powdery. Sift the mixture into a bowl through a large strainer. Discard any fine parts of almond left in the strainer.

STEP 2: Use an electric mixer to whip the egg whites until holding soft peaks. Gradually beat in the superfine sugar, about 1 tablespoon at a time. Beat well after each addition to make a firm and glossy meringue. The meringue should look like shaving cream and hold stiff peaks when the beaters are lifted from the bowl.

STEP 3: Add one-third of the almond mixture to the meringue. Using a spatula, fold the dry mixture into the meringue. Use a circular folding action by running the spatula around the bowl and under the meringue, then folding and cutting through the mixture.

STEP 4: Once all the dry mixture has been folded into the meringue, add the second third of the almond mixture, repeating the folding and cutting action. As more dry ingredients are folded into the meringue it will become firmer.

STEP 5: Add the final third of the almond mixture and repeat the folding and cutting action. Once all the dry ingredients have been incorporated, the batter will be quite firm, so continue mixing until the consistency loosens. The final batter should be smooth and glossy and a thick ribbon of batter should fall slowly from the spatula, leaving a trail for about 30 seconds before disappearing.

Important: Undermixing will result in a batter that is too firm and the macaroons will have peaks. Overmixing will result in a runny batter that will not hold its shape when piped. Check the batter every few turns of the spatula to avoid overmixing.

STEP 6: Line 2 baking sheets with parchment paper. Pour the batter into a large pastry bag fitted with a ½-inch/1-cm tip. Pipe 1¼-inch/3-cm circles onto the prepared baking sheets. Make sure the circles are well spaced. For large macaroons, pipe 2¾-inch/7-cm circles, and, for mini macaroons, pipe ¾-inch/2-cm circles.

STEP 7: Tap the underside of the baking sheet firmly with the palm of your hand or tap onto a work surface to remove any air bubbles and settle any small peaks and bumps. This action also helps the frilly foot (or *pied*) to form during baking. Any peaks still remaining can be flattened by dabbing gently with a wetted fingertip.

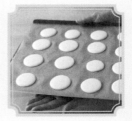

STEP 8: Let the macaroons stand at room temperature for 30 minutes to let the surface of each macaroon dry and form a slight crust. You should be able to gently touch the surface without any batter sticking to your finger.

STEP 9: Bake the macaroons, 1 baking sheet at a time. Check after 5–6 minutes—if they are overbrowning, reduce the oven temperature slightly. The cooking time will be 10–15 minutes, depending on your oven, so check again at 10 minutes. The macaroons are ready when they have a crisp shell and the frilly foot at the bottom does not wobble when the shells are gently lifted from the paper. If the bottoms are still soft or sticky, return the baking sheet to the oven for an additional few minutes, leaving the door ajar.

STEP 10: Let the macaroons cool on the baking sheets for 10 minutes. Carefully peel them away from the parchment paper. Let the macaroons cool completely on a wire rack.

Essential Equipment

Measuring cups
Spoon dry ingredients into the appropriate measuring cup and level off any excess with the straight edge of a knife.

Food processor
In order to achieve a finely ground almond-and-confectioners' sugar mixture you will need a food processor or a large blender with a sharp blade. A coffee or spice grinder is useful for grinding nuts and seeds to flavor the macaroons.

Strainer
To remove any coarse pieces of almond from the processed mixture, a large strainer with medium-fine holes is essential. Sifting the mixture also helps to remove any lumps that may have formed during processing.

Electric mixer
An electric mixer makes light work of whipping egg whites and making meringue. Choose a mixer with at least 3 speed settings.

Spatula
Folding the ground almonds and confectioners' sugar into the meringue is the most vital stage of macaroon making and for this you will need a rubber or silicone spatula with a firm handle and flexible tip.

Baking sheets
It's worth investing in a couple of solid baking sheets that won't buckle in the oven to ensure neatly shaped macaroons. Line with nonstick parchment paper.

Pastry bag and tip
For piping perfect macaroons onto the baking sheet, make sure you have a large-capacity pastry bag. Reusable pliable nylon or plastic-lined cloth pastry bags can be used. A plastic or metal plain tip with a ½-inch/1-cm hole is also needed.

Basic Ingredients

It only takes a few basic ingredients to make simple macaroon shells.

Ground almonds
These give macaroons their slightly chewy texture and nutty flavor. Although it is possible to buy almonds that have already been ground, they need to be processed to a finer texture before using to give a smooth finish to the baked macaroons.

Confectioners' sugar
The ground almonds are processed with confectioners' sugar to create a superfine dry mixture that is easy to fold into the meringue.

Egg whites
In common with any kind of baking, eggs should be used at room temperature when making macaroons. If you have time, separate the eggs a few hours before making the macaroons and let the whites stand in a bowl covered loosely with a paper towel. This lets some moisture evaporate from the whites.

Food colorings
These can be either in gel-paste or liquid form. A small amount of paste will give a good strong color, so add sparingly. If using liquid coloring, whisk it into the meringue a few drops at a time. Adding coloring will create more moisture in the batter, so you may find that brightly colored macaroons will take a few more minutes to bake.

Flavorings
All kinds of flavorings can be used in macaroons, from ground nuts and seeds to citrus rind, spices, coffee, and tea. Add dry flavorings, such as spices, to the almond-and-confectioners' sugar mixture, and liquid or moist flavorings, such as vanilla extract or lemon rind, to the meringue mixture.

Classic Flavors

Vanilla Macaroons

makes 16

¾ cup ground almonds
1 cup confectioners' sugar
2 extra large egg whites
¼ cup superfine sugar
½ tsp vanilla extract

filling

4 tbsp unsalted butter, softened
½ tsp vanilla extract
1 cup confectioners' sugar, sifted

Place the ground almonds and confectioners' sugar in a food processor and process for 15 seconds. Sift the mixture into a bowl. Line 2 baking sheets with parchment paper.

Place the egg whites in a large bowl and whip until holding soft peaks. Gradually beat in the superfine sugar to make a firm, glossy meringue. Beat in the vanilla extract.

Using a spatula, fold the almond mixture into the meringue one-third at a time. When all the dry ingredients are thoroughly incorporated, continue to cut and fold the mixture until it forms a shiny batter with a thick, ribbonlike consistency.

Pour the batter into a pastry bag fitted with a ½-inch/1-cm plain tip. Pipe 32 small circles onto the prepared baking sheets. Tap the baking sheets firmly onto a work surface to remove air bubbles. Let stand at room temperature for 30 minutes. Preheat the oven to 325°F/160°C.

Bake in the preheated oven for 10–15 minutes. Cool for 10 minutes. Carefully peel the macaroons off the parchment paper and let cool completely.

To make the filling, beat the butter and vanilla extract in a bowl until pale and fluffy. Gradually beat in the confectioners' sugar until smooth and creamy. Use to sandwich pairs of macaroons together.

Chocolate Macaroons

makes 16

¾ cup ground almonds

scant 1 cup confectioners' sugar

2 tbsp unsweetened cocoa

2 extra large egg whites

¼ cup superfine sugar

filling

3½ oz/100 g semisweet chocolate, finely chopped

⅔ cup heavy cream

Place the ground almonds, confectioners' sugar, and cocoa in a food processor and process for 15 seconds. Sift the mixture into a bowl. Line 2 baking sheets with parchment paper.

Place the egg whites in a large bowl and whip until holding soft peaks. Gradually beat in the superfine sugar to make a firm, glossy meringue.

Using a spatula, fold the almond mixture into the meringue one-third at a time. When all the dry ingredients are thoroughly incorporated, continue to cut and fold the mixture until it forms a shiny batter with a thick, ribbonlike consistency.

Pour the batter into a pastry bag fitted with a ½-inch/1-cm plain tip. Pipe 32 small circles onto the prepared baking sheets. Tap the baking sheets firmly onto a work surface to remove air bubbles. Let stand at room temperature for 30 minutes. Preheat the oven to 325°F/160°C.

Bake in the preheated oven for 10–15 minutes. Cool for 10 minutes. Carefully peel the macaroons off the parchment paper and let cool completely.

To make the filling, place the chocolate in a heatproof bowl. Heat the cream in a saucepan until just boiling, then pour the hot cream over the chocolate and stir until smooth. Let cool for 15–20 minutes, stirring occasionally, until thickened. Use to sandwich pairs of macaroons together.

Rose Water Macaroons

makes 16

¾ cup ground almonds
1 cup confectioners' sugar
2 extra large egg whites
¼ cup superfine sugar
½ tsp rose water
pink food coloring paste or liquid
1 tbsp candied rose petals

filling
⅔ cup heavy cream
2 tsp rose water

Place the ground almonds and confectioners' sugar in a food processor and process for 15 seconds. Sift the mixture into a bowl. Line 2 baking sheets with parchment paper.

Place the egg whites in a large bowl and whip until holding soft peaks. Gradually beat in the superfine sugar to make a firm, glossy meringue. Beat in the rose water and enough food coloring to give a pale pink color.

Using a spatula, fold the almond mixture into the meringue one-third at a time. When all the dry ingredients are thoroughly incorporated, continue to cut and fold the mixture until it forms a shiny batter with a thick, ribbonlike consistency.

Pour the batter into a pastry bag fitted with a ½-inch/1-cm plain tip. Pipe 32 small circles onto the prepared baking sheets. Tap the baking sheets firmly onto a work surface to remove air bubbles. Top half the macaroons with 2–3 candied rose petals. Let stand at room temperature for 30 minutes. Preheat the oven to 325°F/160°C.

Bake in the preheated oven for 10–15 minutes. Cool for 10 minutes. Carefully peel the macaroons off the parchment paper and let cool completely.

To make the filling, whip the cream and rose water together until holding soft peaks. Use to sandwich pairs of macaroons together.

Pistachio Macaroons

makes 16

½ cup ground almonds

¼ cup finely ground pistachios, plus 2 tbsp finely chopped to decorate

1 cup confectioners' sugar

2 extra large egg whites

¼ cup superfine sugar

green food coloring paste or liquid

filling

6 tbsp unsalted butter, softened

green food coloring paste or liquid

1½ cups confectioners' sugar, sifted

2 tbsp finely chopped pistachios

Place the ground almonds, ground pistachios, and confectioners' sugar in a food processor and process for 15 seconds. Sift the mixture into a bowl. Line 2 baking sheets with parchment paper.

Place the egg whites in a large bowl and whip until holding soft peaks. Gradually beat in the superfine sugar to make a firm, glossy meringue. Beat in enough food coloring to give a pale green color.

Using a spatula, fold the almond mixture into the meringue one-third at a time. When all the dry ingredients are thoroughly incorporated, continue to cut and fold the mixture until it forms a shiny batter with a thick, ribbonlike consistency.

Pour the batter into a pastry bag fitted with a ½-inch/1-cm plain tip. Pipe 32 small circles onto the prepared baking sheets. Tap the baking sheets firmly onto a work surface to remove air bubbles. Sprinkle over the chopped pistachios. Let stand at room temperature for 30 minutes. Preheat the oven to 325°F/160°C.

Bake in the preheated oven for 10–15 minutes. Cool for 10 minutes. Carefully peel the macaroons off the parchment paper and let cool completely.

To make the filling, beat the butter and a little food coloring in a bowl. Gradually beat in the confectioners' sugar until smooth and creamy. Stir in the chopped pistachios. Use to sandwich pairs of macaroons together.

Coffee Cream Macaroons

makes 16

¾ cup ground almonds
1 tsp instant coffee powder
1 cup confectioners' sugar
2 extra large egg whites
¼ cup superfine sugar
1 tbsp lightly crushed sugar crystals

filling
¼ cup cream cheese
2 tbsp unsalted butter, softened
2 tsp strong cold black coffee
1 cup confectioners' sugar, sifted

Place the ground almonds, coffee powder, and confectioners' sugar in a food processor and process for 15 seconds. Sift the mixture into a bowl. Line 2 baking sheets with parchment paper.

Place the egg whites in a large bowl and whip until holding soft peaks. Gradually beat in the superfine sugar to make a firm, glossy meringue.

Using a spatula, fold the almond mixture into the meringue one-third at a time. When all the dry ingredients are thoroughly incorporated, continue to cut and fold the mixture until it forms a shiny batter with a thick, ribbonlike consistency.

Pour the batter into a pastry bag fitted with a ½-inch/1-cm plain tip. Pipe 32 small circles onto the prepared baking sheets. Tap the baking sheets firmly onto a work surface to remove air bubbles. Sprinkle over the sugar crystals. Let stand at room temperature for 30 minutes. Preheat the oven to 325°F/160°C.

Bake in the preheated oven for 10–15 minutes. Cool for 10 minutes. Carefully peel the macaroons off the parchment paper and let cool completely.

To make the filling, place all the ingredients in a bowl and, using an electric mixer, beat until smooth. Use to sandwich pairs of macaroons together.

Lemon Macaroons

makes 16

¾ cup ground almonds
1 cup confectioners' sugar
2 extra large egg whites
¼ cup superfine sugar
finely grated rind of ½ lemon
yellow food coloring paste
or liquid

filling
½ cup mascarpone cheese
finely grated rind of ½ lemon
1 tsp lemon juice
¼ cup lemon curd

Place the ground almonds and confectioners' sugar in a food processor and process for 15 seconds. Sift the mixture into a bowl. Line 2 baking sheets with parchment paper.

Place the egg whites in a large bowl and whip until holding soft peaks. Gradually beat in the superfine sugar to make a firm, glossy meringue. Beat in the lemon rind and enough food coloring to give a bright yellow color.

Using a spatula, fold the almond mixture into the meringue one-third at a time. When all the dry ingredients are thoroughly incorporated, continue to cut and fold the mixture until it forms a shiny batter with a thick, ribbonlike consistency.

Pour the batter into a pastry bag fitted with a ½-inch/1-cm plain tip. Pipe 32 small circles onto the prepared baking sheets. Tap the baking sheets firmly onto a work surface to remove air bubbles. Let stand at room temperature for 30 minutes. Preheat the oven to 325°F/160°C.

Bake in the preheated oven for 10–15 minutes. Cool for 10 minutes. Carefully peel the macaroons off the parchment paper and let cool completely.

To make the filling, beat the mascarpone and lemon rind and juice together until smooth. Spread lemon curd over half the macaroons and the mascarpone mixture over the other half. Carefully sandwich together in pairs.

Hazelnut Chocolate Macaroons

makes 16

½ cup ground almonds

¼ cup finely ground hazelnuts, plus 1 tbsp chopped to decorate

1 cup confectioners' sugar

2 extra large egg whites

¼ cup superfine sugar

generous ⅓ cup hazelnut and chocolate spread

Place the ground almonds, ground hazelnuts, and confectioners' sugar in a food processor and process for 15 seconds. Sift the mixture into a bowl. Line 2 baking sheets with parchment paper.

Place the egg whites in a large bowl and whip until holding soft peaks. Gradually beat in the superfine sugar to make a firm, glossy meringue.

Using a spatula, fold the almond mixture into the meringue one-third at a time. When all the dry ingredients are thoroughly incorporated, continue to cut and fold the mixture until it forms a shiny batter with a thick, ribbonlike consistency.

Pour the batter into a pastry bag fitted with a ½-inch/1-cm plain tip. Pipe 32 small circles onto the prepared baking sheets. Tap the baking sheets firmly onto a work surface to remove air bubbles. Sprinkle over the chopped hazelnuts. Let stand at room temperature for 30 minutes. Preheat the oven to 325°F/160°C.

Bake in the preheated oven for 10–15 minutes. Cool for 10 minutes. Carefully peel the macaroons off the parchment paper and let cool completely.

Sandwich pairs of macaroons together with the hazelnut and chocolate spread.

Fancy Flavors

Saffron & Cardamom Macaroons

makes 16

¾ cup ground almonds

1 cup confectioners' sugar

2 extra large egg whites

¼ tsp crushed saffron strands, plus extra strands to decorate

¼ cup superfine sugar

yellow food coloring paste or liquid

filling

4 tbsp unsalted butter, softened

seeds from 4 cardamom pods, finely crushed

1 cup confectioners' sugar, sifted

Place the ground almonds and confectioners' sugar in a food processor and process for 15 seconds. Sift the mixture into a bowl. Line 2 baking sheets with parchment paper.

Place the egg whites and crushed saffron strands in a large bowl and whip until holding soft peaks. Gradually beat in the superfine sugar to make a firm, glossy meringue. Beat in enough food coloring to give a pale yellow color.

Using a spatula, fold the almond mixture into the meringue one-third at a time. When all the dry ingredients are thoroughly incorporated, continue to cut and fold the mixture until it forms a shiny batter with a thick, ribbonlike consistency.

Pour the batter into a pastry bag fitted with a ½-inch/1-cm plain tip. Pipe 32 small circles onto the prepared baking sheets. Tap the baking sheets firmly onto a work surface to remove air bubbles. Sprinkle over the extra saffron strands. Let stand at room temperature for 30 minutes. Preheat the oven to 325°F/160°C.

Bake in the preheated oven for 10–15 minutes. Cool for 10 minutes. Carefully peel the macaroons off the parchment paper and let cool completely.

To make the filling, beat the butter and cardamom seeds in a bowl until pale and fluffy. Gradually beat in the confectioners' sugar until smooth and creamy. Use to sandwich pairs of macaroons together.

Chocolate Ginger Macaroons

makes 16

¾ cup ground almonds
1 cup confectioners' sugar
1 tsp ground ginger
2 extra large egg whites
¼ cup superfine sugar

filling
2 tbsp unsalted butter
1 tbsp preserved ginger syrup
3 oz/85 g semisweet
chocolate, broken into pieces
¼ cup heavy cream
1 piece preserved ginger,
finely chopped

Place the ground almonds, confectioners' sugar, and ground ginger in a food processor and process for 15 seconds. Sift the mixture into a bowl. Line 2 baking sheets with parchment paper.

Place the egg whites in a large bowl and whip until holding soft peaks. Gradually beat in the superfine sugar to make a firm, glossy meringue.

Using a spatula, fold the almond mixture into the meringue one-third at a time. When all the dry ingredients are thoroughly incorporated, continue to cut and fold the mixture until it forms a shiny batter with a thick, ribbonlike consistency.

Pour the batter into a pastry bag fitted with a ½-inch/1-cm plain tip. Pipe 32 small circles onto the prepared baking sheets. Tap the baking sheets firmly onto a work surface to remove air bubbles. Let stand at room temperature for 30 minutes. Preheat the oven to 325°F/160°C.

Bake in the preheated oven for 10–15 minutes. Cool for 10 minutes. Carefully peel the macaroons off the parchment paper and let cool completely.

To make the filling, melt the butter, ginger syrup, and chocolate in a heatproof bowl set over a pan of simmering water. Remove from the heat and stir in the cream and preserved ginger. Cool for 20 minutes, stirring occasionally, until thickened. Use to sandwich pairs of macaroons together.

Peanut Butter & Jelly Macaroons

makes 16

½ cup ground almonds

¼ cup finely ground unsalted roasted peanuts

1 cup confectioners' sugar

2 extra large egg whites

¼ cup superfine sugar

1 tbsp finely chopped salted peanuts

filling

¼ cup peanut butter

2 tbsp raspberry jelly

Place the ground almonds, ground peanuts, and confectioners' sugar in a food processor and process for 15 seconds. Sift the mixture into a bowl. Line 2 baking sheets with parchment paper.

Place the egg whites in a large bowl and whip until holding soft peaks. Gradually beat in the superfine sugar until to make a firm, glossy meringue.

Using a spatula, fold the almond mixture into the meringue one-third at a time. When all the dry ingredients are thoroughly incorporated, continue to cut and fold the mixture until it forms a shiny batter with a thick, ribbonlike consistency.

Pour the batter into a pastry bag fitted with a ½-inch/1-cm plain tip. Pipe 32 small circles onto the prepared baking sheets. Tap the baking sheets firmly onto a work surface to remove air bubbles. Sprinkle over the salted peanuts. Let stand at room temperature for 30 minutes. Preheat the oven to 325°F/160°C.

Bake in the preheated oven for 10–15 minutes. Cool for 10 minutes. Carefully peel the macaroons off the parchment paper and let cool completely.

Sandwich pairs of macaroons together with the peanut butter and jelly.

Green Tea Macaroons

makes 16

¾ cup ground almonds

1 cup confectioners' sugar,
plus extra for dusting

2 tsp green tea leaves

2 large egg whites

¼ cup superfine sugar

green food coloring paste or
liquid

filling

4 tbsp unsalted butter,
softened

juice and finely grated rind of
½ lemon

1 cup confectioners' sugar,
sifted

Place the ground almonds, confectioners' sugar, and green tea in a food processor and process for 15 seconds. Sift the mixture into a bowl. Line 2 baking sheets with parchment paper.

Place the egg whites in a large bowl and whip until holding soft peaks. Gradually beat in the superfine sugar until to make a firm, glossy meringue. Beat in enough green food coloring to give a pale green color.

Using a spatula, fold the almond mixture into the meringue one-third at a time. When all the dry ingredients are thoroughly incorporated, continue to cut and fold the mixture until it forms a shiny batter with a thick, ribbonlike consistency.

Pour the batter into a pastry bag fitted with a ½-inch/1-cm plain tip. Pipe 32 small circles onto the prepared baking sheets. Tap the baking sheets firmly onto a work surface to remove air bubbles. Let stand at room temperature for 30 minutes. Preheat the oven to 325°F/160°C.

Bake in the preheated oven for 10–15 minutes. Cool for 10 minutes. Carefully peel the macaroons off the parchment paper and let cool completely.

To make the filling, beat the butter and lemon juice and rind in a bowl until pale and fluffy. Gradually beat in the confectioners' sugar until smooth and creamy. Use to sandwich pairs of macaroons together. Dust with confectioners' sugar.

Sesame & Lime Macaroons

makes 16

½ cup ground almonds

3 tbsp finely ground toasted sesame seeds, plus 1 tsp extra to decorate

1 cup confectioners' sugar

2 extra large egg whites

¼ cup superfine sugar

filling

½ cup cream cheese

juice and finely grated rind of ½ lime

2 tbsp confectioners' sugar, sifted

green food coloring paste or liquid

Place the ground almonds, ground sesame seeds, and confectioners' sugar in a food processor and process for 15 seconds. Sift the mixture into a bowl. Line 2 baking sheets with parchment paper.

Place the egg whites in a large bowl and whip until holding soft peaks. Gradually beat in the superfine sugar to make a firm, glossy meringue.

Using a spatula, fold the almond mixture into the meringue one-third at a time. When all the dry ingredients are thoroughly incorporated, continue to cut and fold the mixture until it forms a shiny batter with a thick, ribbonlike consistency.

Pour the batter into a pastry bag fitted with a ½-inch/1-cm plain tip. Pipe 32 small circles onto the prepared baking sheets. Tap the baking sheets firmly onto a work surface to remove air bubbles. Sprinkle over the sesame seeds. Let stand at room temperature for 30 minutes. Preheat the oven to 325°F/160°C.

Bake in the preheated oven for 10–15 minutes. Cool for 10 minutes. Carefully peel the macaroons off the parchment paper and let cool completely.

To make the filling, beat the cream cheese, lime juice and rind, and confectioners' sugar until smooth. Add enough food coloring to give a pale green color. Use to sandwich pairs of macaroons together.

Mint Chocolate Macaroons

makes 16

¾ cup ground almonds

1 cup confectioners' sugar

2 extra large egg whites

¼ cup superfine sugar

1 tsp peppermint extract

green food coloring paste
or liquid

2 tbsp chocolate sprinkles

filling

4 tbsp unsalted butter,
softened

½ cup confectioners' sugar

2 oz/55 g milk chocolate,
melted and cooled for
15 minutes

Place the ground almonds and confectioners' sugar in a food processor and process for 15 seconds. Sift the mixture into a bowl. Line 2 baking sheets with parchment paper.

Place the egg whites in a large bowl and whip until holding soft peaks. Gradually beat in the superfine sugar to make a firm, glossy meringue. Beat in the peppermint extract and enough green food coloring to give a bright green colour.

Using a spatula, fold the almond mixture into the meringue one-third at a time. When all the dry ingredients are thoroughly incorporated, continue to cut and fold the mixture until it forms a shiny batter with a thick, ribbonlike consistency.

Pour the batter into a pastry bag fitted with a ½-inch/1-cm plain tip. Pipe 32 small circles onto the prepared baking sheets. Tap the baking sheets firmly onto a work surface to remove air bubbles. Top with the chocolate sprinkles. Let stand at room temperature for 30 minutes. Preheat the oven to 325°F/160°C.

Bake in the preheated oven for 10–15 minutes. Cool for 10 minutes. Carefully peel the macaroons off the parchment paper and let cool completely.

To make the filling, beat the butter until pale and fluffy. Sift in the confectioners' sugar and beat thoroughly until smooth and creamy, then fold in the melted chocolate. Use to sandwich pairs of macaroons together.

Violet & Lavender Macaroons

makes 16

¾ cup ground almonds
1 cup confectioners' sugar
2 extra large egg whites
¼ cup lavender sugar
violet food coloring paste or liquid
1 tsp candied violets
1 tsp dried lavender

filling
½ cup cream cheese
2 tbsp lavender sugar

Place the ground almonds and confectioners' sugar in a food processor and process for 15 seconds. Sift the mixture into a bowl. Line 2 baking sheets with parchment paper.

Place the egg whites in a large bowl and whip until holding soft peaks. Gradually beat in the lavender sugar until to make a firm, glossy meringue. Beat in enough food coloring to give a pale violet color.

Using a spatula, fold the almond mixture into the meringue one-third at a time. When all the dry ingredients are thoroughly incorporated, continue to cut and fold the mixture until it forms a shiny batter with a thick, ribbonlike consistency.

Pour the batter into a pastry bag fitted with a ½-inch/1-cm plain tip. Pipe 32 small circles onto the prepared baking sheets. Tap the baking sheets firmly onto a work surface to remove air bubbles. Sprinkle over the candied violets and dried lavender. Let stand at room temperature for 30 minutes. Preheat the oven to 325°F/160°C.

Bake in the preheated oven for 10–15 minutes. Cool for 10 minutes. Carefully peel the macaroons off the parchment paper and let cool completely.

To make the filling, beat together the cream cheese and lavender sugar until smooth. Use to sandwich pairs of macaroons together.

Tiramisù Macaroons

makes 16

¾ cup ground almonds
1 tsp instant coffee powder
1 cup confectioners' sugar
2 extra large egg whites
¼ cup superfine sugar
1 tsp unsweetened cocoa

filling
½ cup mascarpone cheese
1 tbsp Marsala wine or sweet sherry
2 tbsp superfine sugar
2 tbsp grated chocolate

Place the ground almonds, coffee powder, and confectioners' sugar in a food processor and process for 15 seconds. Sift the mixture into a bowl. Line 2 baking sheets with parchment paper.

Place the egg whites in a large bowl and whip until holding soft peaks. Gradually beat in the superfine sugar to make a firm, glossy meringue.

Using a spatula, fold the almond mixture into the meringue one-third at a time. When all the dry ingredients are thoroughly incorporated, continue to cut and fold the mixture until it forms a shiny batter with a thick, ribbonlike consistency.

Pour the batter into a pastry bag fitted with a ½-inch/1-cm plain tip. Pipe 32 small circles onto the prepared baking sheets. Tap the baking sheets firmly onto a work surface to remove air bubbles. Sift the cocoa over the macaroons. Let stand at room temperature for 30 minutes. Preheat the oven to 325°F/160°C.

Bake in the preheated oven for 10–15 minutes. Cool for 10 minutes. Carefully peel the macaroons off the parchment paper and let cool completely.

To make the filling, beat the mascarpone, Marsala wine, and superfine sugar together until smooth. Spread the mascarpone mixture over half the macaroons, sprinkle over the grated chocolate, and top with the remaining macaroons.

44

Fruity Flavors

Strawberry Macaroons

makes 16

¾ cup ground almonds

1 cup confectioners' sugar,
plus extra for dusting

2 extra large egg whites

¼ cup superfine sugar

pink food coloring paste
or liquid

filling

4 tbsp unsalted butter,
softened

½ tsp vanilla extract

1 cup confectioners'
sugar, sifted

4 strawberries, hulled and
finely chopped

Place the ground almonds and confectioners' sugar in a food processor and process for 15 seconds. Sift the mixture into a bowl. Line 2 baking sheets with parchment paper.

Place the egg whites in a large bowl and whip until holding soft peaks. Gradually beat in the superfine sugar to make a firm, glossy meringue. Beat in enough food coloring to give a bright pink color.

Using a spatula, fold the almond mixture into the meringue one-third at a time. When all the dry ingredients are thoroughly incorporated, continue to cut and fold the mixture until it forms a shiny batter with a thick, ribbonlike consistency.

Pour the batter into a pastry bag fitted with a ½-inch/1-cm plain tip. Pipe 32 small circles onto the prepared baking sheets. Tap the baking sheets firmly onto a work surface to remove air bubbles. Let stand at room temperature for 30 minutes. Preheat the oven to 325°F/160°C.

Bake in the preheated oven for 10–15 minutes. Cool for 10 minutes. Carefully peel the macaroons off the parchment paper and let cool completely.

To make the filling, beat the butter and vanilla extract in a bowl until pale and fluffy. Gradually beat in the confectioners' sugar until smooth and creamy. Fold in the strawberries. Use to sandwich pairs of macaroons together. Dust with confectioners' sugar.

Tangy Orange Macaroons

makes 16

¾ cup ground almonds

1 cup confectioners' sugar

2 extra large egg whites

¼ cup superfine sugar

2 tsp finely grated orange rind

orange food coloring paste or liquid

¼ cup orange marmalade

Place the ground almonds and confectioners' sugar in a food processor and process for 15 seconds. Sift the mixture into a bowl. Line 2 baking sheets with parchment paper.

Place the egg whites in a large bowl and whip until holding soft peaks. Gradually beat in the superfine sugar to make a firm, glossy meringue. Beat in the orange rind and enough food coloring to give a bright orange color.

Using a spatula, fold the almond mixture into the meringue one-third at a time. When all the dry ingredients are thoroughly incorporated, continue to cut and fold the mixture until it forms a shiny batter with a thick, ribbonlike consistency.

Pour the batter into a pastry bag fitted with a ½-inch/1-cm plain tip. Pipe 32 small circles onto the prepared baking sheets. Tap the baking sheets firmly onto a work surface to remove air bubbles. Let stand at room temperature for 30 minutes. Preheat the oven to 325°F/160°C.

Bake in the preheated oven for 10–15 minutes. Cool for 10 minutes. Carefully peel the macaroons off the parchment paper and let cool completely.

Sandwich pairs of macaroons together with the marmalade.

Spiced Apple Macaroons

makes 16

¾ cup ground almonds
1 cup confectioners' sugar
1 tsp ground cinnamon
2 extra large egg whites
¼ cup superfine sugar
½ tsp freshly grated nutmeg

filling
1 lb/450 g baking apples, peeled, cored, and chopped
3 tbsp superfine sugar
1 tbsp water

Place the ground almonds, confectioners' sugar, and cinnamon in a food processor and process for 15 seconds. Sift the mixture into a bowl. Line 2 baking sheets with parchment paper.

Place the egg whites in a large bowl and whip until holding soft peaks. Gradually beat in the superfine sugar to make a firm, glossy meringue.

Using a spatula, fold the almond mixture into the meringue one-third at a time. When all the dry ingredients are thoroughly incorporated, continue to cut and fold the mixture until it forms a shiny batter with a thick, ribbonlike consistency.

Pour the batter into a pastry bag fitted with a ½-inch/1-cm plain tip. Pipe 32 small circles onto the prepared baking sheets. Tap the baking sheets firmly onto a work surface to remove air bubbles. Sprinkle with the grated nutmeg. Let stand at room temperature for 30 minutes. Preheat the oven to 325°F/160°C.

Bake in the preheated oven for 10–15 minutes. Cool for 10 minutes. Carefully peel the macaroons off the parchment paper and let cool completely.

To make the filling, place the apples, superfine sugar, and water in a small pan. Cover and simmer for 10 minutes, until soft. Mash with a fork to make a puree, then let cool. Use to sandwich pairs of macaroons together.

Nutty Banana & Toffee Macaroons

makes 16

½ cup ground almonds

¼ cup finely ground pecans, plus 1 tbsp chopped to decorate

1 cup confectioners' sugar

2 extra large egg whites

¼ cup superfine sugar

filling

½ small banana, finely chopped

¼ cup dulce de leche (toffee sauce)

Place the ground almonds, ground pecans, and confectioners' sugar in a food processor and process for 15 seconds. Sift the mixture into a bowl. Line 2 baking sheets with parchment paper.

Place the egg whites in a large bowl and whip until holding soft peaks. Gradually beat in the superfine sugar until you have a firm, glossy meringue.

Using a spatula, fold the almond mixture into the meringue one-third at a time. When all the dry ingredients are thoroughly incorporated, continue to cut and fold the mixture until it forms a shiny batter with a thick, ribbonlike consistency.

Pour the batter into a pastry bag fitted with a ½-inch/1-cm plain tip. Pipe 32 small circles onto the prepared baking sheets. Tap the baking sheets firmly onto a work surface to remove air bubbles. Sprinkle over the chopped pecans. Let stand at room temperature for 30 minutes. Preheat the oven to 325°F/160°C.

Bake in the preheated oven for 10–15 minutes. Cool for 10 minutes. Carefully peel the macaroons off the parchment paper and let cool completely.

To make the filling, mix together the banana and dulce de leche. Use to sandwich pairs of macaroons together.

Mango & Passion Fruit Macaroons

makes 16

¾ cup ground almonds

1 cup confectioners' sugar

2 extra large egg whites

¼ cup superfine sugar

½ tsp vanilla extract

yellow food coloring paste
or liquid

1 piece plumped dried mango,
finely chopped

filling

⅔ cup heavy cream

3 tbsp mango puree

2 tbsp passion fruit pulp

Place the ground almonds and confectioners' sugar in a food processor and process for 15 seconds. Sift the mixture into a bowl. Line 2 baking sheets with parchment paper.

Place the egg whites in a large bowl and whip until holding soft peaks. Gradually beat in the superfine sugar to make a firm, glossy meringue. Beat in the vanilla extract and enough food coloring to give a bright yellow color.

Using a spatula, fold the almond mixture into the meringue one-third at a time. When all the dry ingredients are thoroughly incorporated, continue to cut and fold the mixture until it forms a shiny batter with a thick, ribbonlike consistency.

Pour the batter into a pastry bag fitted with a ½-inch/1-cm plain tip. Pipe 32 small circles onto the prepared baking sheets. Tap the baking sheets firmly onto a work surface to remove air bubbles. Top with the dried mango. Let stand at room temperature for 30 minutes. Preheat the oven to 325°F/160°C.

Bake in the preheated oven for 10–15 minutes. Cool for 10 minutes. Carefully peel the macaroons off the parchment paper and let cool completely.

To make the filling, whip the cream until holding soft peaks, then fold in the mango puree and passion fruit pulp. Use to sandwich pairs of macaroons together.

Blueberry Cheesecake Macaroons

makes 16

¾ cup ground almonds
1 cup confectioners' sugar
2 extra large egg whites
¼ cup superfine sugar
½ tsp vanilla extract
blue food coloring paste
or liquid

filling
½ cup cream cheese
2 tbsp sour cream
1 tbsp confectioners' sugar
generous ½ cup blueberries

Place the ground almonds and confectioners' sugar in a food processor and process for 15 seconds. Sift the mixture into a bowl. Line 2 baking sheets with baking paper.

Place the egg whites in a large bowl and whip until holding soft peaks. Gradually beat in the superfine sugar to make a firm, glossy meringue. Beat in the vanilla extract and enough food coloring to give a bright blue color.

Using a spatula, fold the almond mixture into the meringue one-third at a time. When all the dry ingredients are thoroughly incorporated, continue to cut and fold the mixture until it forms a shiny batter with a thick, ribbonlike consistency.

Pour the batter into a pastry bag fitted with a ½-inch/1-cm plain tip. Pipe 32 small circles onto the prepared baking sheets. Tap the baking sheets firmly onto a work surface to remove air bubbles. Let stand at room temperature for 30 minutes. Preheat the oven to 325°F/160°C.

Bake in the preheated oven for 10–15 minutes. Cool for 10 minutes. Carefully peel the macaroons off the parchment paper and let cool completely.

To make the filling, beat the cream cheese, sour cream, and confectioners' sugar together until smooth. Lightly crush the blueberries and fold into the cream cheese mixture. Use to sandwich pairs of macaroons together.

Raspberry Ripple Macaroons

makes 16

¾ cup ground almonds
1 cup confectioners' sugar
2 extra large egg whites
¼ cup superfine sugar
pink food coloring paste or
liquid

filling

⅔ cup heavy cream
1 tsp vanilla extract
3 tbsp raspberry jelly

Place the ground almonds and confectioners' sugar in a food processor and process for 15 seconds. Sift the mixture into a bowl. Line 2 baking sheets with parchment paper.

Place the egg whites in a large bowl and whip until holding soft peaks. Gradually beat in the superfine sugar to make a firm, glossy meringue. Beat in enough food coloring to give a bright pink color.

Using a spatula, fold the almond mixture into the meringue one-third at a time. When all the dry ingredients are thoroughly incorporated, continue to cut and fold the mixture until it forms a shiny batter with a thick, ribbonlike consistency.

Pour the batter into a pastry bag fitted with a ½-inch/1-cm plain tip. Pipe 32 small circles onto the prepared baking sheets. Tap the baking sheets firmly onto a work surface to remove air bubbles. Use the tip of a toothpick to swirl a little food coloring through the top of each macaroon. Let stand at room temperature for 30 minutes. Preheat the oven to 325°F/160°C.

Bake in the preheated oven for 10–15 minutes. Cool for 10 minutes. Carefully peel the macaroons off the parchment paper and let cool completely.

To make the filling, whip the cream and vanilla extract together until holding soft peaks. Sandwich pairs of macaroons together with the vanilla cream and jelly.

Coconut & Pineapple Macaroons

makes 16

½ cup ground almonds

¼ cup finely ground unsweetened coconut, plus 2 tbsp toasted to decorate

1 cup confectioners' sugar

2 extra large egg whites

¼ cup superfine sugar

filling

4 tbsp unsalted butter, softened

2 tsp pineapple juice

1 cup confectioners' sugar, sifted

2 rings canned pineapple, drained and finely chopped

Place the ground almonds, ground coconut, and confectioners' sugar in a food processor and process for 15 seconds. Sift the mixture into a bowl. Line 2 baking sheets with parchment paper.

Place the egg whites in a large bowl and whip until holding soft peaks. Gradually beat in the superfine sugar until you have a firm, glossy meringue.

Using a spatula, fold the almond mixture into the meringue one-third at a time. When all the dry ingredients are thoroughly incorporated, continue to cut and fold the mixture until it forms a shiny batter with a thick, ribbonlike consistency.

Pour the batter into a pastry bag fitted with a ½-inch/1-cm plain tip. Pipe 32 small circles onto the prepared baking sheets. Tap the baking sheets firmly onto a work surface to remove air bubbles. Sprinkle over the toasted coconut. Let stand at room temperature for 30 minutes. Preheat the oven to 325°F/160°C.

Bake in the preheated oven for 10–15 minutes. Cool for 10 minutes. Carefully peel the macaroons off the parchment paper and let cool completely.

To make the filling, beat the butter and pineapple juice in a bowl until pale and fluffy. Gradually beat in the confectioners' sugar until smooth and creamy, then fold in the chopped pineapple. Use to sandwich pairs of macaroons together.

Something Special

Sweetheart Macaroons

makes 6

¾ cup ground almonds
1 cup confectioners' sugar
2 extra large egg whites
¼ cup superfine sugar
pink food coloring paste or
liquid

filling

4 oz/115 g white chocolate,
finely chopped
1¼ cups heavy cream

Place the ground almonds and confectioners' sugar in a food processor and process for 15 seconds. Sift the mixture into a bowl. Line 2 baking sheets with parchment paper and, using a 2¾-inch/7-cm heart-shape cookie cutter, mark 12 heart shapes on the paper.

Place the egg whites in a large bowl and whip until holding soft peaks. Gradually beat in the superfine sugar to make a firm, glossy meringue. Beat in enough food coloring to give a pale pink color.

Using a spatula, fold the almond mixture into the meringue one-third at a time. When all the dry ingredients are thoroughly incorporated, continue to cut and fold the mixture until it forms a shiny batter with a thick, ribbonlike consistency.

Pour the batter into a pastry bag fitted with a ½-inch/1-cm plain tip. Pipe heart shapes onto the prepared baking sheets. Tap the baking sheets firmly onto a work surface to remove air bubbles. Let stand at room temperature for 30 minutes. Preheat the oven to 325°F/160°C.

Bake in the preheated oven for 15–20 minutes. Cool for 10 minutes. Carefully peel the macaroons off the parchment paper and let cool completely.

To make the filling, place the chocolate in a heatproof bowl. Heat half the cream in a pan until boiling, then pour over the chocolate and stir until smooth. Let cool completely. Whip the remaining cream until holding soft peaks and fold into the chocolate mixture. Use to sandwich pairs of macaroons together.

Summer Berry Macaroons

makes 6

¾ cup ground almonds
1 cup confectioners' sugar
2 extra large egg whites
¼ cup superfine sugar
fresh mint sprigs, to decorate

filling
⅔ cup heavy cream
2 tbsp lemon curd
generous ¾ cup hulled and
sliced strawberries, plus extra
whole strawberries
to decorate
generous ¾ cup raspberries
2 tbsp confectioners' sugar

Place the ground almonds and confectioners' sugar in a food processor and process for 15 seconds. Sift the mixture into a bowl. Line 2 baking sheets with parchment paper.

Place the egg whites in a large bowl and whip until holding soft peaks. Gradually beat in the superfine sugar to make a firm, glossy meringue.

Using a spatula, fold the almond mixture into the meringue one-third at a time. When all the dry ingredients are thoroughly incorporated, continue to cut and fold the mixture until it forms a shiny batter with a thick, ribbonlike consistency.

Pour the batter into a piping bag fitted with a ½-inch/1-cm plain tip. Pipe 12 large circles onto the prepared baking sheets. Tap the baking sheets firmly onto a work surface to remove air bubbles. Let stand at room temperature for 30 minutes. Preheat the oven to 325°F/160°C.

Bake in the preheated oven for 15–20 minutes. Cool for 10 minutes. Carefully peel the macaroons off the parchment paper and let cool completely.

To make the filling, whip the cream until holding soft peaks, then fold in the lemon curd. Top half the macaroon shells with the lemon cream and arrange two-thirds of the berries on top. Puree the remaining berries with the confectioners' sugar. Drizzle a little of the puree over the berries and top with the remaining macaroons. Serve decorated with mint sprigs and whole strawberries.

Mont Blanc Macaroons

makes 6

¾ cup ground almonds

scant 1 cup confectioners'
sugar, plus extra for dusting

2 tbsp unsweetened cocoa

2 extra large egg whites

¼ cup superfine sugar

filling

1 cup heavy cream

¼ cup sweetened chestnut
puree

2 tbsp semisweet chocolate
shavings

Place the ground almonds, confectioners' sugar, and cocoa in a food processor and process for 15 seconds. Sift the mixture into a bowl. Line 2 baking sheets with parchment paper.

Place the egg whites in a large bowl and whip until holding soft peaks. Gradually beat in the superfine sugar to make a firm, glossy meringue.

Using a spatula, fold the almond mixture into the meringue one-third at a time. When all the dry ingredients are thoroughly incorporated, continue to cut and fold the mixture until it forms a shiny batter with a thick, ribbonlike consistency.

Pour the batter into a pastry bag fitted with a ½-inch/1-cm plain tip. Pipe 12 large circles onto the prepared baking sheets. Tap the baking sheets firmly onto a work surface to remove air bubbles. Let stand at room temperature for 30 minutes. Preheat the oven to 325°F/160°C.

Bake in the preheated oven for 15–20 minutes. Cool for 10 minutes. Carefully peel the macaroons off the parchment paper and let cool completely.

To make the filling, whip the cream until holding soft peaks and fold into the chestnut puree. Pipe the chestnut mixture onto half the macaroons. Top with chocolate shavings and the remaining macaroon shells. Serve dusted with confectioners' sugar.

Christmas Macaroons

makes 16

¾ cup ground almonds

1 cup confectioners' sugar

1 tsp ground allspice

2 extra large egg whites

¼ cup superfine sugar

½ tsp freshly grated nutmeg

1 tsp gold dragées

filling

4 tbsp unsalted butter, softened

juice and finely grated rind of ½ orange

1 tsp ground allspice

1 cup confectioners' sugar, sifted

2 tbsp finely chopped candied cherries

Place the ground almonds, confectioners' sugar, and allspice in a food processor and process for 15 seconds. Sift the mixture into a bowl. Line 2 baking sheets with parchment paper.

Place the egg whites in a large bowl and whip until holding soft peaks. Gradually beat in the superfine sugar to make a firm, glossy meringue.

Using a spatula, fold the almond mixture into the meringue one-third at a time. When all the dry ingredients are thoroughly incorporated, continue to cut and fold the mixture until it forms a shiny batter with a thick, ribbonlike consistency.

Pour the batter into a pastry bag fitted with a ½-inch/1-cm plain tip. Pipe 32 small circles onto the prepared baking sheets. Tap the baking sheets firmly onto a work surface to remove air bubbles. Sprinkle half the macaroons with the grated nutmeg and the gold dragées. Let stand at room temperature for 30 minutes. Preheat the oven to 325°F/160°C.

Bake in the preheated oven for 10–15 minutes. Cool for 10 minutes. Carefully peel the macaroons off the parchment paper and let cool completely.

To make the filling, beat the butter and orange juice and rind in a bowl until fluffy. Gradually beat in the allspice and confectioners' sugar until smooth and creamy. Fold in the candied cherries. Use to sandwich pairs of macaroons together.

Rum Truffle Macaroons

makes 16

¾ cup ground almonds

1 cup confectioners' sugar, plus extra for dusting

2 extra large egg whites

¼ cup superfine sugar

½ tsp vanilla extract

unsweetened cocoa, for dusting

filling

4 oz/115 g semisweet chocolate, broken into pieces

2 tbsp unsalted butter

scant ⅓ cup heavy cream

1 tbsp rum

Place the ground almonds and confectioners' sugar in a food processor and process for 15 seconds. Sift the mixture into a bowl. Line 2 baking sheets with parchment paper.

Place the egg whites in a large bowl and whip until holding soft peaks. Gradually beat in the superfine sugar to make a firm, glossy meringue. Beat in the vanilla extract.

Using a spatula, fold the almond mixture into the meringue one-third at a time. When all the dry ingredients are thoroughly incorporated, continue to cut and fold the mixture until it forms a shiny batter with a thick, ribbonlike consistency.

Pour the batter into a pastry bag fitted with a ½-inch/1-cm plain tip. Pipe 32 small circles onto the prepared baking sheets. Tap the baking sheets firmly onto a work surface to remove air bubbles. Let stand at room temperature for 30 minutes. Preheat the oven to 325°F/160°C.

Bake in the preheated oven for 10–15 minutes. Cool for 10 minutes. Carefully peel the macaroons off the parchment paper and let cool completely.

To make the filling, melt the chocolate and butter in a heatproof bowl set over a pan of simmering water. Remove from the heat and stir in the cream and rum. Cool for 10 minutes, then chill in the refrigerator for 30–40 minutes, until thick enough to spread. Use to sandwich pairs of macaroons together. Dust half of each macaroon with confectioners' sugar and the other half with cocoa.

Mini Macaroons

makes 30

¾ cup ground almonds
1 cup confectioners' sugar
2 extra large egg whites
¼ cup superfine sugar
½ tsp vanilla extract
colored sprinkles, to decorate

filling
generous ⅓ cup unsalted butter, softened
1 tsp vanilla extract
1½ cups confectioners' sugar, sifted
pink, yellow, and green food coloring pastes or liquids

Place the ground almonds and confectioners' sugar in a food processor and process for 15 seconds. Sift the mixture into a bowl. Line 2 baking sheets with parchment paper.

Place the egg whites in a large bowl and whip until holding soft peaks. Gradually beat in the superfine sugar to make a firm, glossy meringue. Beat in the vanilla extract.

Using a spatula, fold the almond mixture into the meringue one-third at a time. When all the dry ingredients are thoroughly incorporated, continue to cut and fold the mixture until it forms a shiny batter with a thick, ribbonlike consistency.

Pour the batter into a pastry bag fitted with a ½-inch/1-cm plain tip. Pipe 60 tiny circles onto the prepared baking sheets. Tap the baking sheets firmly onto a work surface to remove air bubbles. Top with the sprinkles. Let stand at room temperature for 30 minutes. Preheat the oven to 325°F/160°C.

Bake in the preheated oven for 10–14 minutes. Cool for 10 minutes. Carefully peel the macaroons off the parchment paper and let cool completely.

To make the filling, beat the butter and vanilla extract in a bowl until pale and fluffy. Gradually beat in the confectioners' sugar until smooth and creamy. Divide the buttercream into 3 bowls and color each with pink, yellow, or green food coloring. Use to sandwich pairs of macaroons together.

Chocolate Macaroon Gâteau

3 oz/85 g semisweet chocolate, broken into pieces

¾ cup unsalted butter, softened, plus extra for greasing

scant 1 cup superfine sugar

scant 1⅓ cups self-rising flour

½ tsp baking powder

3 extra large eggs, beaten

2 tbsp unsweetened cocoa

14 chocolate macaroon shells (see page 16)

white and semisweet chocolate curls, to decorate

frosting & filling

6 oz/175 g semisweet chocolate, finely chopped

2 cups heavy cream

Preheat the oven to 350°F/180°C. Grease two 9-inch/23-cm round cake pans and line the bottoms with parchment paper. Melt the chocolate in a heatproof bowl set over a pan of simmering water. Remove from the heat and let cool, stirring occasionally.

Place the butter, sugar, flour, baking powder, eggs, and cocoa in a large bowl and, using an electric mixer, beat until smooth and creamy. Fold in the melted chocolate.

Spoon the batter into the prepared pans and level the surfaces. Bake in the preheated oven for 20–25 minutes, or until risen and just firm to the touch. Let cool in the pans for 5 minutes, then turn out and let cool completely.

For the frosting, place the chocolate in a heatproof bowl. Heat 1¼ cups of the cream in a pan until just boiling, then pour the hot cream over the chocolate and stir until smooth. Let cool for 20–30 minutes, stirring occasionally, until thick enough to spread. Whip the remaining cream until holding soft peaks.

Sandwich the cakes together with one-third of the frosting and the whipped cream. Spread the remaining frosting over the top and sides of the cake. Gently press the macaroon shells onto the frosting around the sides of the cake. Decorate the top with chocolate curls.